Expressions From Lancashire
Edited by Angela Fairbrace

First published in Great Britain in 2007 by:
Young Writers
Remus House
Coltsfoot Drive
Peterborough
PE2 9JX
Telephone: 01733 890066
Website: www.youngwriters.co.uk

All Rights Reserved

© *Copyright Contributors 2007*

SB ISBN 978-1 84431 290 0

Foreword

Young Writers was established in 1991 and has been passionately devoted to the promotion of reading and writing in children and young adults ever since. The quest continues today. Young Writers remains as committed to the nurturing of poetic and literary talent as ever.

This year's Young Writers competition has proven as vibrant and dynamic as ever and we are delighted to present a showcase of the best poetry from across the UK and in some cases overseas. Each poem has been selected from a wealth of *Little Laureates* entries before ultimately being published in this, our sixteenth primary school poetry series.

Once again, we have been supremely impressed by the overall quality of the entries we have received. The imagination, energy and creativity which has gone into each young writer's entry made choosing the poems a challenging and often difficult but ultimately hugely rewarding task - the general high standard of the work submitted ensured this opportunity to bring their poetry to a larger appreciative audience.

We sincerely hope you are pleased with this final collection and that you will enjoy *Little Laureates Expressions From Lancashire* for many years to come.

Contents

Blacko CP School
Levi Nicholson (11)	1
Louise Frost (10)	2
Laura Tomlinson (11)	3
Ellis Dickinson (10)	4
Megan Wych (10)	6
Georgia Sharples (10)	8
Ben Anson (11)	9

East Crompton St George's Primary School
Joe Gloster (8)	10
Mason Harper (8)	11
Erika May (8)	12
Billy George (8)	13
Jessica O'Sullivan (8)	14
Sam Hewitt (8)	15
Daniel Cooke (8)	16
Samantha Richardson (8)	17
Samantha Woodworth (8)	18
Alexander Richardson (8)	19
Ben Robinson (8)	20
Beth Dunleavy (8)	21
Hannah Hussain (7)	22
Jack Leach (7)	23
Danielle Wray (8)	24
Molly Needham (8)	25

Garswood CP School
Samuel Birchall (10)	26
Sophie Spanner (10)	27
Emma Porter (9)	28
Megan Fawn (8)	29
Rhianna Hough (9)	30
Luke Pickavance (9)	31
Rebecca Eaves (9)	32
Olivia Dermott (10)	33
Megan Brown (10)	34
Chelsea Chesworth (10)	35

Amy Green (8) — 36
Amie Hopper (9) — 37
Courtney Hitchmough (9) — 38

Helmshore Primary School
Louise Pyrah (9) — 39
Charlie Hall (9) — 40
Ellie Harris (9) — 41
Owen Lord (8) — 42
Andrew Mousley (8) — 43
Samuel Charles (8) — 44
James Harding (9) — 45
Nicole Jackson (9) — 46
Nicole Marcroft (9) — 47
David Holt (8) — 48
Peter Connelly (9) — 49
Amy Hogarth (8) — 50
Alice Tiler (8) — 51
Lydia Flavell (10) — 52
Jessica Haynes (10) & Imogen Lyth (9) — 53
Edward Bowers & Oliver Holdsworth-Miller (9) — 54
Thomas Harding (9) — 55
Alex Jeffrey (10) — 56
Oliver Myers (9) — 57
Megan Ashwell (10) — 58
Lauren Johnson (10) — 59
Ahmad Beitelmal (11) — 60
Alex Bowers (10) — 61
Robbie Mawdsley (10) — 62
Katie Fowler (10) — 63
Callum Johnson (11) — 64
Helena Hannah-Shelton (11) — 65
Daniel Wilson (11) — 66
George Peel (10) — 67
Nicholas Holloway (7) — 68
Alex Higgins (7) — 69
Jessica Nelson (8) — 70
Zain Ishaque (7) — 71
Amy Green (8) — 72
McLaren Ashworth (8) — 73
Chloe Johnson (8) — 74

Presley Morris (8)	75
Thomas Robertshaw (8)	76
Hannah Shatliff (8)	77
Isabelle Rapley (8)	78
Eleanor Harrison (7)	79
Emma Burnside (8)	80
Katie Prosser (8)	81
Nezar Beitelmal (7)	82
Jasmine Strangeway (8)	83
Ryan Crofts (8)	84
Toby Wilkinson (11)	85
Brodie McEvoy (10)	86
Shannon Higginbotham (11)	87
Nathan Shaughnessy (11)	88
Jack Bradley (11)	89
Rhys Heap (11)	90
Brodie Georgina Glynn (11)	91
Paige Ward (11)	92
Jonathan Ford (10)	93
Rebecca Swales (11)	94
Paige Hardman (11)	95
Elisha Hackett (11)	96
Lee Bates (10)	97
Callum Watson (10)	98
Luke Wood (10)	99
Molly Harris (9)	100
Tabitha Cross (10)	101
Olivia Harrison (10)	102
Ashleigh Brooks (10)	103
Tom Cross (10)	104
Laura Alice Jackson (10)	105
Jack Tiler (10)	106
Elizabeth Hollberry-Goddard (10)	107
Katie Kendall (9)	108
Selene Bridge (10)	109
Nick Cooper (10)	110
Hannah Lundberg-Bury (10)	111
Lauren Watson (9)	112
Connor Walsh (9)	113
Kim Smith (10)	114
Matthew Densfield (10)	115
Lauren Haworth (9)	116

Elspeth Lord (9)	117
Harriet Carruthers (9)	118
Toby Kay (10)	119
Millie Keys (9)	120
Zak Drake (10)	121
John Stuart (10)	122
Morgan Bacon (8)	123
Harry Yates (8)	124
George Carpenter (7)	125
Hannah Thornton (8)	126
Heidi Wilson (8)	127
Sarah Jessica Russell (8)	128
Josef Ratcliffe (8)	129
Amy Mastyla (7)	130
Courtney Lord (8)	131
Mollie Haynes (8)	132
Courtney Hardman (7)	133
Josh Haddy (8)	134
Jamie Gamble (8)	135
Erin Dempsey-McWade (7)	136
Oliver Lord (8)	137
Sean Frith (9)	138
Fraser Chapman (8)	139
Daniel Rice (8)	140

Orrell Lamberhead Green CP School

Chloe Geraghty (10)	141
Connor Johnson (10)	142
Alix Carr (10)	143
David Fagan (10)	144
Shannon Hurley (10)	145
Callum Taylor (9)	146
Jade Hurley (10)	147
Georgia King (10)	148
Andrew Morris (10)	149
Jack Boyle (9)	150
Michael Jones (10)	151

Pinfold Primary School

Nicole Amy Wilson (10)	152

Jake Daniel Higham (10)	153
Shevana Kent (9)	154

St Andrew's Over Hulton CE Primary School, Bolton

Elliot Holt (8)	155
Peter Gradwell (8)	156
Lucy Waddington (9)	157
Alex Latham (9)	158
Alex Cooper (9)	159
Amy Grundy (9)	160
Ellie Shawcross (9)	161
Brandon Melia (9)	162
Rachel Peacock (9)	163
Jasmine Delvard (9)	164
Amy Neill (9)	165

St Francis of Assisi Primary School, Skelmersdale

Nicola Robinson (10)	166
Andrew Moss (10)	167
Bethany Rimmet (9)	168
Courtney Rowlands (9)	169
Matthew Wise (9)	170
Emma Millar (9)	171
Abbey Cash-Francis (10)	172

St Matthews CE Primary School, Bolton

Faeema Kakuji (11)	173
Liam Conroy (10)	174

The Poems

It's As Easy As . . .

It's as easy as breathing on Mars
Or sending your sheep to the stars.

It's as easy as getting a peanut to play hockey
Or getting a horse to enter a race with no jockey.

It's as easy as talking to a mime
Or trying to stop the passing of time.

It's as easy as getting a penguin to fly or
Going to Oddies and not buying a pie.

It's as easy as making conversation with a duck
Or trying to catch a toddler when you're stuck in some muck.

It's as easy as flying your kite with no wind
Or getting a priest to say you've not sinned.

It's as easy as getting a snail to win a race
Or getting the police to have a chase.

It's as easy as lifting a tractor's tyre
Or using a piece of plastic wire.

It's as easy as this, it's no piece of cake
Trying to get rid of this toffee toothache.

Levi Nicholson (11)
Blacko CP School

It's As Easy As . . .

It's as easy as getting a belly button to sing
Or for the sun to wear a diamond ring.

It's as easy as making a nose be happy
Or getting a cat to wear a nappy.

It's as easy as making a tree speak
Or allowing a wrestler to be weak.

It's as easy as three times nine to be two
Or making a kite start to moo.

It's as easy as turning an orang-utan pink
Or getting a perfume to really stink.

It's as easy as getting a fire to be cold
Or making plastic grow mould.

It's as easy as getting a witch to giggle
Or making a worm not wiggle.

It's as easy as getting the Queen to make her own meals
Or getting a shark to move on wheels.

It's as easy as this, it's no piece of cake
Trying to get rid of my toffee toothache.

Louise Frost (10)
Blacko CP School

As Easy As . . .

It's as easy as making a clock give up time,
Or making a pencil case riddle and rhyme.

It's as easy as making a baby be old,
Or the golden sun to be terribly cold.

It's as easy as making a snail win a race,
Or finding a flower with a face.

It's as easy as money making people poor,
Or a greyhound dog turning into a door.

It's as easy as making a fish breathe air,
Or telling a bald man to grow back his hair.

It's as easy as seeing a scary, white ghost,
Or juggling oranges standing on a post.

It's as easy as telling a cube to roll,
Or telling a pig to give birth to a foal.

It's as easy as getting a brick wall to speak,
Or to want to eat sprouts every day of the week.

It's as easy as this, it's no piece of cake,
Trying to get rid of my toothache!

Laura Tomlinson (11)
Blacko CP School

I'm Strolling With My . . .

I'm strolling
With my gorilla

I'm strolling
With my gorilla

Later in the evening
When the sun starts to set
My gorilla and me
Decide to get wet

So we go for a walk
As late as can be
Now no one can see him
As we swim in the sea

And I'm strolling
With my gorilla

I'm strolling
With my gorilla

I look at my gorilla
As he grows and grows
By eating and eating
With his gleaming claws

In the blink of an eye
My gorilla runs free
Better go find him
But where could he be?

When I'm strolling
With my gorilla

I'm strolling
With my gorilla

I call the police
As quick as I can
Then they track him down
Arghhh! He's trying to kill a man

We travel back home
He's ready for bed
I'm glad he's asleep
Because he looks half dead

I'm strolling
With my gorilla

Still strolling
With my gorilla.

Ellis Dickinson (10)
Blacko CP School

I'm Walking With My Chinchilla

I'm walking
With my chinchilla

I'm walking
With my chinchilla

In the afternoon
At about half-past three
We go to sleep
My chinchilla and me

She wakes up before me
And tries to wake me up
But the only thing that wakes me
Is tea in a cup!

So I start walking
With my chinchilla

Still walking
With my chinchilla

We walk to a restaurant
In the middle of town
But Jinni doesn't like it
And gives me a frown

She's got a bit giddy
So I put her on a lead
She pulls a bit and very nearly weed

I'm walking
With my chinchilla

I'm walking
With my chinchilla

So we go swimming
In a swimming pool
And she sees some food
That makes her drool

I take her to the shop
For some food
I get her some chocolate
And she is in a bad mood

So I'm walking
With my chinchilla

Still walking
With my chinchilla

As we walk back home
To our house
She falls asleep
And is as quiet as a mouse.

Megan Wych (10)
Blacko CP School

I'm Hopping With My Monkey

I'm hopping with my monkey
I'm hopping with my monkey

Late at night
At half-past ten
Me and my monkey
Went to get a pen

We went to bed
My monkey and me
We went outside
And we saw a tree

I'm hopping with my monkey
I'm hopping with my monkey.

Georgia Sharples (10)
Blacko CP School

It's As Easy As . . .

It's as easy as getting the Queen to fly in the air
Or convincing Tony Blair

It's as easy as having a fourth wish
Or greeting a swordfish

It's as easy as getting Presley to cut his hair bald
Or, in Australia, catching a cold

It's as easy as getting a snail to produce a tear
Or reading Shakespeare

It's as easy as depriving a dragon of his fire
Or trying to melt wire

It's as easy as touching the sun
Or resisting a freshly iced bun

It's as easy as drinking metal
Or eating a rose petal

It's as easy as stretching set salt bread
Or rising from the dead

It's as easy as this, it's no toothache
Trying to eat my hard rock cakes.

Ben Anson (11)
Blacko CP School

Dangerous Dragon

D anger lurks in the mist. Black dragon will attack
R iders ride into the mist
A ttack the black dragon
G rowls from the dragon as he is slaughtered
O n the ground lay the dragon
N o one had any fear anymore.

Joe Gloster (8)
East Crompton St George's Primary School

Adventure

A dventures are the best
D o you like them?
V ery spooky things
E ven spooky bats
N ine lives for me!
T ough, big antelope
U nicorns all around
R eckless dinosaurs
E ven tusky elephants.

Mason Harper (8)
East Crompton St George's Primary School

Animal

A ntelope walking around the forest
N ewt swimming in the stream
I nsects jumping about
M ice scuttling
A lligator's snapping jaws
L ions roaring loudly.

Erika May (8)
East Crompton St George's Primary School

Football

F ootball's great
O ops! I hit my manager
O h, a goal!
T ook a shot
B ack to the second half
A super goal!
L ike the best footballer ever
L ittle power on that shot.

Billy George (8)
East Crompton St George's Primary School

Dragons

D ragons are heroes
R iders are cool!
A ll dragons blow fire
G eorge and the Dragon
O range dragons, red dragons and blue dragons
N ot a dragon left
S top the dragon destroying the village.

Jessica O'Sullivan (8)
East Crompton St George's Primary School

Dragons

Dragons like to blow fire
Dragons like to live in a cold castle
Dragons like to eat beautiful princesses
Dragons like to look at some treasure while guarding princesses
Dragons need to be slayed by dragon slayers.

Sam Hewitt (8)
East Crompton St George's Primary School

Superheroes!

S uperheroes soar
U p, up and away
P ower punch
E asy assaults
R unning like lightning

H eroes have super strength
E ven flight!
R ay beams
O pen vaults
E xtra powers
S uperheroes are the best!

Daniel Cooke (8)
East Crompton St George's Primary School

A Topsy-Turvy Land

Giraffes as small as butterflies
Mice as big as elephants
Hamsters as hard as hippos
Rabbit's tail as hard as a rhino's tusk
Dogs don't chase cats
Cats chase dogs!
Mice eat lions
Worms as straight as bookmarks
Bookmarks as wiggly as worms
And that is what it is like in Topsy-Turvy Land.

Samantha Richardson (8)
East Crompton St George's Primary School

Rabbits

R abbit food is nice
A tail as fluffy as a little baby guinea pig
B anana is nice for their food
B ottles are full of water
I stroke my rabbit every day
T witch their noses
S wish goes the water down to their tummy.

Samantha Woodworth (8)
East Crompton St George's Primary School

Football

F eet kick the ball up high
O ops! I tackled my own player
O h no, I missed!
T ime for half-time
B all goes flying in the air
A man scored a goal
L ike my star player
L ike that guy over there.

Alexander Richardson (8)
East Crompton St George's Primary School

Football

F ootball is great
O wn goal!
O h, I scored a goal
T ake a penalty against the goalie
B reak time
A ll the crowd goes wild
L ovely crowd
L ight ball.

Ben Robinson (8)
East Crompton St George's Primary School

Rounders

R un round the square
O h, I got a rounder
U nlucky, the other team won
N o way I'm going to bat
D o you like rounders?
E nd base you go and hit it
R ounders is good
S ome people are in rounders.

Beth Dunleavy (8)
East Crompton St George's Primary School

Animals

Squirrels are climbing
Dolphins are jumping
Dogs are walking
Cats are pouncing
Kangaroos are leaping
Mice are squeaking
Rats are screeching
Tadpoles are splashing
Snails are slithering
Elephants are thumping
Lions are roaring
Bees are buzzing
Wasps are stinging.

Hannah Hussain (7)
East Crompton St George's Primary School

Football

F eel, kick the ball far or you can pass
O ops! I got a red card
O pen net, nearly scored a goal
T he ball is very hard
B alls go very high when you kick them
A m I the captain today?
L ampard scored the winning goal
L atics are the best!

Jack Leach (7)
East Crompton St George's Primary School

Gymnasts

Gymnasts like to do giants on the bars
Gymnasts like to stick to all the moves on the beam
Gymnasts like to go on the power track and do flicks to the end
Gymnasts like to go on rebound and do all the moves
Gymnasts like to go on the tumble track and do round-off flick tuck
Gymnasts like to go on the floor and do their floor routines.

Danielle Wray (8)
East Crompton St George's Primary School

Netball

N etball practice every week.
E nergy for the team.
T ake the ball away from her.
B all goes in the net.
A way from the net.
L arge improvement for the players.
L ook around for your teammate.

Molly Needham (8)
East Crompton St George's Primary School

Dragon

Burning throat,
With gliding wings,
Tail that's hooked like a fishing rod,
Travel in the dark where knights fear to tread
And eat all the children
Who are tucked up in bed.
What am I?
A: A dragon.

Samuel Birchall (10)
Garswood CP School

Emotions

I am angry, so vicious and bright red,
I am upset, so down, so distraught,
I am stroppy, I am stomping everywhere,
I am miserable, so upset,
I am amazed, so smiley, so filled with sparkles
I am so attractive, so charming and cheerful
I am happy, like a supersonic cowgirl.
Yeah, that's me!

Sophie Spanner (10)
Garswood CP School

What Emotion Am I?

When the moon is out
And Mum turns out the light,
I'm scared out of my skin,
In this moonlit night.

Midnight's coming closer,
I can feel it in my soul,
It's burning very hard,
Like a lot of coal.

The chimes are ringing slowly,
It's going through the house,
Everyone can hear it,
Even a tiny mouse.

Day is coming closer,
I try, I try, I try,
Something is fluttering,
Oh, it's lots of pretty butterflies.
I'm scared!

Emma Porter (9)
Garswood CP School

My Cat Benjy

Hi,
My name is Benjy and I am a cat.
I love playing with things that dangle down.

I am a ginger tom
And I came from
The Cat's Protection League.

I eat dried and mushy food.
I have pointed ears
And a *very* rough tongue!

I have multicoloured eyes
And a stripy, fluffy tail.
I have white, spiky whiskers.

That's me done!

Megan Fawn (8)
Garswood CP School

Wild Weather

The tornado was as cold as ice,
It made me feel grumpy and scared
As it picked up everything in its path.
It made me feel cold and lonely.
The scorching sun was scarring my skin
As it shone on my head and I felt boiling.
The snowstorm made me feel frozen.
It was as white as a piece of paper
And the only place I wanted to be was at home.

I felt sad.

Rhianna Hough (9)
Garswood CP School

Weather

Sun is as warm as a hot desert,
Boiling and scorching.

Rain is as dull as the night sky mist,
Cold on my face.

Lightning is as fast as a cheetah,
Bright and dangerous.

Fog is dark and thick like the narrow mist,
Frightening and shaking.

Our weather.

Luke Pickavance (9)
Garswood CP School

Witch

A witch is black and green, with her big black cat.
She's thunder and lightning on the move.
She reminds me of a spooky black castle.
I hear her crazy, cruel cackle.
I smell her horrid smell, like stale sardines and toad's skin.
If I touched her skin I think it would feel so lumpy and bumpy,
I would faint at her sight.

Rebecca Eaves (9)
Garswood CP School

The Park

I feel the soft, green grass in-between my fingers,
Blowing from side to side,
I see happy, smiley faces all around me.
I smell the fascinating flowers on the tender, soft ground.
I can taste soft, creamy strawberry ice cream,
Melting in my wonderfully warm mouth,
I can hear the lovely, beautiful birds tweeting around
The wonderful, joyful place.
Oh, how I love the park.

Olivia Dermott (10)
Garswood CP School

Dreams

I jump into bed,
Snuggle down,
Happy and warm.
I am as sleepy as a baby,
I dream I visit a place,
Where only I go,
A special place,
Where monkeys and people
Play in the soft sand.
Big sandcastles to climb inside.
Dream over.
I wake up in my soft bed
And stretch!

Megan Brown (10)
Garswood CP School

Sunshine

Smiley, hot sunshine,
Shining on me,
As I lie on the grass
Watching the fluffy clouds go by,
Making shapes out of them.
Oh look, I can see a pig,
Now there's a dog fetching a bone,
A little girl getting tickled by her mum and dad.
But that's just my imagination.
Oh, I do wish it was like this every day,
Playing in the sunshine,
Surrounded by a family that loves me.

Chelsea Chesworth (10)
Garswood CP School

My Pony

Tiny and grey,
Just gorgeous!
Bites when angry,
Likes eating carrots.
Loves rolling over in the green field.
Lives in a small stable.
Makes me feel special.
When I ride, I'm free,
In a paddock full of jumps.
That's my pony.

Amy Green (8)
Garswood CP School

Blue

Blue is the colour of the soft, sparkly sky.
Blue is the colour of my beautiful eyes.
Blue is the colour of the deep, dark sea.
Blue is the colour that is special to me.

Amie Hopper (9)
Garswood CP School

My Little Sister

My little sister makes me as angry as a lion
When she pulls my hair,
But,
My little sister makes me as happy as sunshine
When she hugs me tight.
My little sister makes me as excited as can be
When she says, 'I love you, Courtney!'

Courtney Hitchmough (9)
Garswood CP School

Night Noises

After I'm in bed
I hear doors creaking
I hear phones ringing
I hear people sneaking

Outside my house
With my window open
I hear cars going past

I hear bats swooping by my window
I listen to them all
In the garden they are swooping
On my garden wall

I hear someone in the bathroom
I hear water dripping
I hear someone talking
I hear people skipping.

Louise Pyrah (9)
Helmshore Primary School

Night Noises

After I'm in bed
I hear doors creaking
I hear the phone ringing
I hear the baby crying

I hear my dog barking
I hear fireworks going off
I hear cars going past
I hear my fish moving

I hear people speaking
I hear people walking past
I hear children's voices
I hear the wind going past.

Charlie Hall (9)
Helmshore Primary School

Night Noises

After I'm in bed
I hear doors creaking
I get out of bed
Then I hear some people speaking

Outside my house
I hear cars going past
With my window open
They are going very fast

I hear someone in the bathroom
I hear water dripping
I hear people talking
I hear people skipping.

Ellie Harris (9)
Helmshore Primary School

Night Noises

After I'm in bed
I hear my door creaking
And my dog barking
And my sister sneaking out.

I hear my TV on
And my brother snoring
I hear my clock ticking
And a lion roaring.

I hear my fish splashing
And my toilet flushing
And my tap dripping
I hear the wind dashing.

I hear my dog barking
And fireworks banging
And I hear my radiator cracking
And my floor creaking.

Owen Lord (8)
Helmshore Primary School

Night Noises

After I'm in bed,
When it's really dark,
I like to listen
To my neighbour's dog bark.

There's something wrong with my house,
The taps are always leaking,
There's rattling in my bathroom
And the stairs are always creaking.

Andrew Mousley (8)
Helmshore Primary School

Night Noises

After I'm in bed
When all creatures come out
I like to hear these noises
Like water dripping from the spout.

When bats soar past my window
I like to hear owls hooting
Because it sounds like singing in the night
And when cars come past my window
They all start to toot.

In the night I hear the sound of doors
Starting to creak
In the night I hear cats prowling
I also hear pipes clanking
And then I hear the wind howling.

When I'm asleep
When the sun rises there is light
These noises are very strange
They are the noises of the night.

Samuel Charles (8)
Helmshore Primary School

Night Noises

After I'm in bed,
At night,
I turn around
And hear a fright

Wind wailing in the sky
Loud footsteps at the door
Pipes tapping up and up
This is what I saw

Leaves whistling above
Cars shooting past
In silence I hear
Birds going very fast

Owls and foxes
In the darkness of the night
The baby is crying
Then I see a speck of light.

James Harding (9)
Helmshore Primary School

Night Noises

After I'm in bed
I hear my brother snoring
And all the way downstairs
I hear some water pouring.

I try to get to sleep
But I can hear the tap dripping
Whilst next door
They might even be flipping.

Everyone is sleeping
And everything is quiet and still
And sometimes, just sometimes
I can hear the wheel from the mill.

Nicole Jackson (9)
Helmshore Primary School

Night Noises

After I'm in bed
I can't get to sleep
I hear a noise
I hear a song called Little Bo Peep.

I hear the branches tapping on my window
And my sister's sneezing
My mum and Karl talking
And it's boring.

I hear a toilet flushing
And next-door's dog barking
And cars zooming
And it's very dark.

Nicole Marcroft (9)
Helmshore Primary School

Night Noises

After I am in bed, I hear water dripping
From my mum running a bath
And I hear my dad snoring
Louder than a sheep bleating.
When I'm in bed I can hear the wind
Howling in the middle of the night.
I can hear my mum and dad talking or arguing.

David Holt (8)
Helmshore Primary School

Night Noises

After I'm in bed
I just can't go to sleep
So I listen to the night noises
When my doors creak

The *bang, bang, bang* of the pipes
In my bed
The screech of cats outside my window
And the flash of car lights going

These are the night noises that I hear.

Peter Connelly (9)
Helmshore Primary School

Night Noises

After I'm in bed,
This is what I do,
I always like to listen to
The noises of the night.
My brother does it too.

This is what I hear,
I hear a distant sound of cars
And planes zooming by.
Here are the noises,
This is what they are:

Dogs barking, cats miaowing,
These are noises of the night.
Frogs croaking all the time,
The stars giving so much light.

Now it's almost light,
The noise dies down,
Everyone's waking up,
Everyone's rushing around.

Amy Hogarth (8)
Helmshore Primary School

Night Noises

After I was in bed,
I struggled to get to sleep.
Something was tapping on my window,
I went to have a peek.

I got back into bed,
I heard a bang outside my room.
I went downstairs,
All the dishes had shattered - *clang!*

Alice Tiler (8)
Helmshore Primary School

Night Noises

N is for night, when I'm in bed
I is for the illusions of the dark
G is for ghosts that come out at night
H is for the howling wind
T is for the tangerine-coloured street light outside

N is for night, when I'm in bed
O is for the other orange street light outside
I is for *I'm scared of the dark*
S is for sounds of thunder and lightning
E is for the exciting wind whistling
S is for the shadow of the moon riding by.

Lydia Flavell (10)
Helmshore Primary School

Night Noises

After I'm in bed
And there isn't any light,
I look out of the window
And it gives me a big fright.

Trees are swaying madly,
Cats are slowly creeping,
I'm getting scared quite badly,
While Mum and Dad are sleeping.

I can hear a man shouting,
He is calling out my name,
I am really getting scared now
And feeling lots of pain.

The shadow of my disco ball,
Shining on my door,
Looks like a man walking
On my purple floor.

I can hear the beating of the rain
Upon my window ledge,
I can see something in the big oak tree
That is behind my garden hedge.

After I'm in bed
And there isn't any light,
I look out of the window,
Holding my teddy tight.

Jessica Haynes (10) & Imogen Lyth (9)
Helmshore Primary School

Night Noises

After I'm in bed
And there isn't any light,
I can see the stars in the sky
And the moon riding by.

I can hear the whistling in the night,
Cats screeching, dogs barking,
They give me a terrible fright.

The tap, tap, tapping of a woodpecker,
Sitting in a tree,
I can see them all,
Clear and free to me.

From my window I can see,
The whole world before me,
The sun setting in the west,
What a lovely sight it is.

I can see the shadows dancing in the dark,
The TV swaying,
A crystal moonbeam shining
As my dog begins to bark.

After I'm in bed
And there isn't any light,
I cuddle up to Teddy
And I cuddle him tight.

Edward Bowers & Oliver Holdsworth-Miller (9)
Helmshore Primary School

Night Noises

After I'm in bed
And there isn't any light,
I like to lie and listen
To the noises of the night

The whistling of the kettle
Going off at night,
The dogs barking loudly
They give me a fright!

All day long I'm happy
But then at night I'm not,
The baby's soiled its nappy
And is crying in its cot!

The traffic lights outside
They seem very bright,
In amongst the noises
The noises of the night!

Thomas Harding (9)
Helmshore Primary School

Night Noises

After I'm in bed
And there isn't any light,
I sit up and listen
To the noises of the night.

The owls are hooting
I hear the tapping on my windowpane,
The whistle of the wind
And the light, gentle rain.

The ghostly shadow of the tree
Beneath a beautiful, black sky,
Sends a shiver down my spine
I listen as I lie.

After I'm in bed
And there isn't any light,
I sit up
And listen to the noises of the night.

Alex Jeffrey (10)
Helmshore Primary School

Night Noises

After I'm in bed
And there isn't any light,
I can see the moon outside
It's shining really bright.

The hooting of an owl
Outside on a tree,
The wind is carrying its noise
All the way to me.

The rain is beating down
Spooky shadows from a tree,
The crackling thunder, really, really loud
The moon blotted out by a gigantic cloud!

After I'm in bed
And there isn't any light,
I like to snuggle up to Ted
It makes me feel alright.

Oliver Myers (9)
Helmshore Primary School

Night Noises

After I'm in bed
And there isn't any light,
A clap of thunder wakes me
And it gives me a fright.

After I'm in bed
And the shadows are awake,
I hear a scream from the TV
And the tension I can't take.

After I'm in bed,
The burning whiff of toast,
Floating up the stairs,
These smells scare me the most.

After I'm in bed,
The lightning flashes brightly,
The rain hammers down,
I hug my teddy tightly.

After I'm in bed
And there isn't any light,
I like to lie and listen
To the noises of the night.

Megan Ashwell (10)
Helmshore Primary School

Night Noises

After I'm in bed
And there isn't any light
I like to sit and listen
To the noises of the night.

A peaceful owl hooting
Beneath the twinkling stars
The soothing sound of branches
The zooming sound of cars.

The dark sky above me
A rustle of leaves in the rain
The wind blows harder
Brushing the windowpane.

In my comfy bed
I hold my pillow tight
I feel safe and warm
With the noises of the night.

Lauren Johnson (10)
Helmshore Primary School

In Case Of War

In case of war, think of cannons,
In case of cannons, think of tanks,
In case of tanks, think of destruction,
In case of destruction, think of ruins,
In case of ruins, think of wrecks,
In case of wrecks, think of ships,
In case of ships, think of battleships,
In case of battleships, think of sinking,
In case of sinking, think of drowning,
In case of drowning, think of help,
In case of help, think of ambulances,
In case of ambulances, think of doctors,
In case of doctors, think of hospitals,
In case of hospitals, think of saving lives,
In case of saving lives, think of chemicals,
In case of chemicals, think of gunpowder,
In case of gunpowder, think of bullets,
In case of bullets, think of shooting,
In case of shooting, think of murder,
In case of murder, think of war.

Ahmad Beitelmal (11)
Helmshore Primary School

Forgiveness

In case of forgiveness, think of righting wrong,
In case of righting wrong, think of doing wrong,
In case of doing wrong, think of fighting,
In case of fighting, think of chaos,
In case of chaos, think of blood,
In case of blood, think of death,
In case of death, think of murder,
In case of murder, think of investigation,
In case of investigation, think of court,
In case of court, think of doing wrong,
In case of doing wrong, think of righting wrong,
In case of righting wrong, think of forgiveness.

Alex Bowers (10)
Helmshore Primary School

In Case Of Freedom

In case of freedom, think of outlaws,
In case of outlaws, think of Robin Hood,
In case of Robin Hood, think of arrows,
In case of arrows, think of wood,
In case of wood, think of forests,
In case of forests, think of bugs,
In case of bugs, think of nature,
In case of nature, think of relaxing,
In case of relaxing, think of quiet,
In case of quiet, think of a mouse,
In case of a mouse, think of running.
In case of running, think of being chased,
In case of being chased, think of getting away,
In case of getting away, think of freedom,
In case of freedom, think of outlaws.

Robbie Mawdsley (10)
Helmshore Primary School

Happiness

In case of happiness, think of laughter,
In case of laughter, think of friendship,
In case of friendship, think of friends,
In case of friends, think of fun,
In case of fun, think of theme parks,
In case of theme parks, think of rides,
In case of rides, think of fast,
In case of fast, think of planes,
In case of planes, think of holidays,
In case of holidays, think of families,
In case of families, think of enjoyment,
In case of enjoyment, think of happiness.

Katie Fowler (10)
Helmshore Primary School

Blood

In case of blood, think of murder,
In case of murder, think of peril,
In case of peril, think of torture,
In case of torture, think of malice,
In case of malice, think of pain,
In case of pain, think of wounds,
In case of wounds, think of flesh,
In case of flesh, think of red,
In case of red, think of sauce,
In case of sauce, think of tomato,
In case of tomato, think of seed,
In case of seed, think of reproduction,
In case of reproduction, think of death,
In case of death, think of blood,
In case of blood, think of murder.

Callum Johnson (11)
Helmshore Primary School

In Case Of Sadness

In case of sadness, think of blue,
In case of blue, think of blood,
In case of blood, think of war,
In case of war, think of death,
In case of death, think of Hell,
In case of Hell, think of chaos,
In case of chaos, think of hope,
In case of hope, think of children,
In case of children, think of smiles,
In case of smiles, think of happiness,
In case of happiness, think of tears,
In case of tears, think of frowns,
In case of frowns, think of glum,
In case of glum, think of sadness,
In case of sadness, think of blue.

Helena Hannah-Shelton (11)
Helmshore Primary School

In Case Of Life

In case of life, think of birth,
In case of birth, think of crying,
In case of crying, think of growing up,
In case of growing up, think of talking,
In case of talking, think of training,
In case of training, think of bikes,
In case of bikes, think of school,
In case of school, think of friends,
In case of friends, think of teenagers,
In case of teenagers, think of adulthood,
In case of adulthood, think of cars,
In case of cars, think of tests,
In case of tests, think of love,
In case of love, think of elder,
In case of elder, think of death,
In case of death, think of life.

Daniel Wilson (11)
Helmshore Primary School

In Case Of War

In case of war, think of guns,
In case of guns, think of bombs,
In case of bombs, think of terror,
In case of terror, think of blood,
In case of blood, think of paint,
In case of paint, think of reception,
In case of reception, think of playing,
In case of playing, think of friends,
In case of friends, think of laughter,
In case of laughter, think of sadness,
In case of sadness, think of war,
In case of war, think of guns.

George Peel (10)
Helmshore Primary School

Surprised

S urprised is when you get something unexpected
U nder the Christmas tree there are lots
R eading the gift card on the surprises
P resents are given to you by people who love you
R ed is for surprises
I like surprises
S ometimes I am surprised
E xcited by the surprise
D on't know who sent the surprise.

Nicholas Holloway (7)
Helmshore Primary School

Angry

A nger is when you feel sad
N ever feeling happy
G oing somewhere where you don't want to go
R ed is the colour for anger
Y ou're angry with a friend.

Alex Higgins (7)
Helmshore Primary School

Brave

B lue whales having a fight
R ays stinging anything or anyone
A pples that have been poisoned
V olcanoes erupt when I'm climbing up them
E lastic bands springing in my face.

Jessica Nelson (8)
Helmshore Primary School

Happy

H appy is when you play with your friends
A nd when you go to JJB Soccer Dome
P eas make you healthy
P eacocks going up, up to the sky
Y ou're very proud of yourself.

Zain Ishaque (7)
Helmshore Primary School

Nervous

N ervous is when you can't do a thing.
E ver been bullied in front of your friends?
R unning a race and you lose.
V iolet is the colour of nervous.
O ven sets on fire because of you.
U sing stabilisers.
S neaking into assembly.

Amy Green (8)
Helmshore Primary School

Happy

H appy at school
A nd at home as well.
P retty hair you have.
P rize you can win.
Y ou look at the clock.

McLaren Ashworth (8)
Helmshore Primary School

Happy

H appy is good.
A lways sunny.
P laying in the park.
P retty flowers in the garden.
Y ellow butterflies.

Chloe Johnson (8)
Helmshore Primary School

Proud

P roud is when you do your homework.
R escue a dog when you are out.
O n the bus and you win a game.
U ndo a knot in your laces.
D id your test and got 30/30.

Presley Morris (8)
Helmshore Primary School

Scared

S cared is when someone is going to beat you up.
C ar crash.
A robbery in your house.
R unning for your life.
E xciting, a fire.
D ie in three weeks.

Thomas Robertshaw (8)
Helmshore Primary School

Angry

A ngry is when people are arguing.
N aughty people kicking each other.
G ran in hospital very ill.
R eally red is Uncle Bill.
Y elling people all around.

Hannah Shatliff (8)
Helmshore Primary School

Scared

S cared is when a monster is in your house.
C reaking floorboards in a haunted room.
A ghost ride and a monster on it with you.
R obber in your house.
E xciting, a big fire.
D ead and sad.

Isabelle Rapley (8)
Helmshore Primary School

Happy

H appy is when you're excited
A nd it is really fun.
P oppies in my garden.
P uppies are jumping because it's Christmas.
Y ellow daffodils in the sunshine.

Eleanor Harrison (7)
Helmshore Primary School

Happy

H appy is when I play with my best friend.
A lways a rainbow to make me happy.
P retty poppies.
P ink lilies in a pot.
Y ellow butterflies flying in the sky.

Emma Burnside (8)
Helmshore Primary School

Happy

H appy is when you are enjoying yourself.
A lways lucky.
P laying at my friend's home.
P arking to go to a party.
Y ellow dress.

Katie Prosser (8)
Helmshore Primary School

Fear

F ear is when you are turning to the dark side.
E ven when you're happy you can still feel fear.
A lways scared.
R unning for your life.

Nezar Beitelmal (7)
Helmshore Primary School

Angry

A ngry is scary.
N obody is happy.
G rumpy is cool.
R apid volcano being nasty.
Y ou're angry, that's good.

Jasmine Strangeway (8)
Helmshore Primary School

Excited

E xcited is when you eat more food.
X -ray on my tummy.
C an't find me, I'm on my swing.
I ce is chilly.
T ingling with excitement.
E ating my favourite food.
D ad coming home from work.

Ryan Crofts (8)
Helmshore Primary School

In Case Of Football

In case of football, think of goals.
In case of goals, think of dreams.
In case of dreams, think of your bed.
In case of your bed, think of comfort.
In case of comfort, think of hot chocolate.
In case of hot chocolate, think of tea.
In case of tea, think of India.
In case of India, think of children.
In case of children, think of hunger.
In case of hunger, think of death.
In case of death, think of George Best.
In case of George Best, think of football legends.
In case of football legends, think of David Beckham.
In case of David Beckham, think of football.
In case of football, think of goals.

Toby Wilkinson (11)
Helmshore Primary School

In Case Of War

In case of war, think of death.
In case of death, think of love.
In case of love, think of sharing.
In case of sharing, think of money.
In case of money, think of happiness.
In case of happiness, think of relationship.
In case of relationship, think of marriage.
In case of marriage, think of reproduction.
In case of reproduction, think of life.
In case of life, think of valuables.
In case of valuables, think of rings.
In case of rings, think of earrings.
In case of earrings think of ears.
In case of ears, think of humans.
In case of humans, think of children.
In case of children, think of protection.
In case of protection think of armour.
In case of armour, think of war.
In case of war, think of death.

Brodie McEvoy (10)
Helmshore Primary School

In Case Of Childhood

In case of childhood, think of fun.
In case of fun, think of games.
In case of games, think of dares,
In case of dares, think of laughter.
In case of laughter, think of jokes.
In case of jokes, think of comedy.
In case of comedy, think of comedians.
In case of comedians, think of clubs.
In case of clubs, think of becoming older.
In case of older, think of love.
In case of love, think of marriage.
In case of marriage, think of settling down.
In case of settling down, think of your heart.
In case of heart, don't break it.
In case of broken heart, think of good memories.
In case of good memories, think of childhood.
In case of childhood, think of fun.
In case of fun, think of games.

Shannon Higginbotham (11)
Helmshore Primary School

In Case Of War

In case of war, think of fighting.
In case of fighting, think of death.
In case of death, think of tears.
In case of tears, think of sadness.
In case of sadness, think of broken hearts.
In case of broken hearts, think of being alone.
In case of being alone, think of one.
In case of one, think of many.
In case of many, think of families.
In case of families, think of marriage.
In case of marriage, think of children.
In case of children, think of joy.
In case of joy, think of fun.
In case of fun, think of friends.
In case of friends, think of happiness.
In case of happiness, think of grace.
In case of grace, think of respect.
In case of respect, think of peace.
In case of peace, think of friendship.
In case of friendship, think of arguments.
In case of arguments, think of war.
In case of war, think of fighting.

Nathan Shaughnessy (11)
Helmshore Primary School

In Case Of Murder

In case of murder, think of guns.
In case of guns, think of bullets.
In case of bullets, think of life.
In case of life, think of childhood.
In case of childhood, think of happiness.
In case of happiness, think of comedy.
In case of comedy, think of Peter Kay.
In case of Peter Kay, think of arenas.
In case of arenas, think of laughter.
In case of laughter, think of victory.
In case of victory, think of football.
In case of football, think of riots.
In case of riots, think of police.
In case of police, think of tear gas.
In case of tear gas, think of tears.
In case of tears, think of death.
In case of death, think of murder.
In case of murder, think of guns.

Jack Bradley (11)
Helmshore Primary School

In Case Of Children

In case of children, think of toys.
In case of toys, think of playing.
In case of playing, think of safe.
In case of safe, think of valuables.
In case of valuables, think of sentiment.
In case of sentiment, think of emotions.
In case of emotions, think of death.
In case of death, think of bodies.
In case of bodies, think of attraction.
In case of attraction, think of relationship.
In case of relationship, think of reproduction.
In case of reproduction, think of children.
In case of children, think of toys.

Rhys Heap (11)
Helmshore Primary School

In Case Of Love

In case of love, think of passion.
In case of passion, think of hearts.
In case of hearts, think of flowers.
In case of flowers, think of death.
In case of death, think of graves.
In case of graves, think of stars.
In case of stars, think of planets.
In case of planets, think of Earth.
In case of Earth, think of humans.
In case of humans, think of relationships.
In case of relationships, think of admiration.
In case of admiration, think of love.
In case of love, think of passion.

Brodie Georgina Glynn (11)
Helmshore Primary School

In Case Of Sisters

In case of sisters, think of anger.
In case of anger, think of frustration.
In case of frustration, think of fights.
In case of fights, think of war.
In case of war, think of death.
In case of death, think of crying.
In case of crying, think of tissues.
In case of tissues, think of paper.
In case of paper, think of trees.
In case of trees, think of flowers.
In case of flowers, think of graves.
In case of graves, think of sadness.
In case of sadness, think of smacking.
In case of smacking, think of sisters.
In case of sisters, think of anger.

Paige Ward (11)
Helmshore Primary School

In Case Of War

In case of war, think of death.
In case of death, think of guns.
In case of guns, think of tears.
In case of tears, think of upset.
In case of upset, think of feelings.
In case of feelings, think of comedy.
In case of comedy, think of Lee Evans.
In case of Lee Evans, think of joy.
In case of joy, think of happiness.
In case of happiness, think of fun.
In case of fun, think of stars.
In case of stars, think of humans.
In case of humans, think of death.
In case of death, think of war.

Jonathan Ford (10)
Helmshore Primary School

In Case Of Love

In case of love, think of giving.
In case of giving, think of sharing.
In case of sharing, think of passion.
In case of passion, think of relationship.
In case of relationship, think of devotion.
In case of devotion, think of hate.
In case of hate, think of deplore.
In case of deplore, think of dislike.
In case of dislike, think of heartbroken.
In case of heartbroken, think of crying.
In case of crying, think of tears.
In case of tears, think of water.
In case of water, think of flowers.
In case of flowers, think of love.
In case of love, think of giving.

Rebecca Swales (11)
Helmshore Primary School

In Case Of War

In case of war, think of death.
In case of death, think of murder.
In case of murder, think of shooting.
In case of shooting, think of blood.
In case of blood, think of tears.
In case of tears, think of helping.
In case of helping, think of friends.
In case of friends, think of friendship.
In case of friendship, think of disappointment.
In case of disappointment, think of sorrow.
In case of sorrow, think of hatred.
In case of hatred, think of shouting.
In case of shouting, think of blood.
In case of blood, think of war.
In case of war, think of death.
In case of death, think of murder.

Paige Hardman (11)
Helmshore Primary School

In Case Of Friendship

In case of friendship, think of friends.
In case of friends, think of love.
In case of love, think of joy.
In case of joy, think of Peter Kay.
In case of Peter Kay, think of laughter.
In case of laughter, think of crying.
In case of crying, think of happiness.
In case of happiness, think of fun.
In case of fun, think of playing.
In case of playing, think of arguments.
In case of arguments, think of sharing.
In case of sharing, think of friendship.
In case of friendship, think of friends.

Elisha Hackett (11)
Helmshore Primary School

In Case Of Friendship

In case of friendship, think of friends.
In case of friends, think of playing.
In case of playing, think of fun.
In case of fun, think of happiness.
In case of happiness, think of trust.
In case of trust, think of sharing.
In case of sharing, think of feelings.
In case of feelings, think of death.
In case of death, think of war.
In case of war, think of winning.
In case of winning, think of friendship.
In case of friendship, think of friends.

Lee Bates (10)
Helmshore Primary School

In Case Of School

In case of school, think of education.
In case of education, think of work.
In case of work, think of jobs.
In case of jobs, think of tasks
In case of tasks, think of glory.
In case of glory, think of achievement.
In case of achievement, think of pride.
In case of pride, think of others.
In case of others, think of friends.
In case of friends, think of friendship.
In case of friendship, think of laughter.
In case of laughter, think of jokes.
In case of jokes, think of sharing.
In case of sharing, think of happiness.
In case of happiness, think of learning.
In case of learning, think of school.
In case of school, think of education.

Callum Watson (10)
Helmshore Primary School

Night Noises

I lie awake in bed
And there is no light.
I like to lie and listen
For the noises of the night.

The rustling of branches,
The faint burrowing of moles,
The cats creeping round
And the squeaking of the voles.

The pitter-patter of rain on the window,
The quacking of the ducks,
The creaking of my brother's bed
And the squelching of feet in muck.

The boom of gates being shut by the wind,
The mooing of the cows,
The vacant creak of rusty farm equipment
And the cats' miaow.

I love the day
And the sunlight
But I also love to lie and listen
For the noises of the night.

Luke Wood (10)
Helmshore Primary School

Night Noises

While I'm in bed,
And it isn't very bright,
I like to stay and listen,
To the noises of the night.

The hoot of the owl
Sitting on the wall,
The violent sounds of gushing winds
And my cat playing with the ball.

The pound of hailstones,
Fewer cars passing by,
The little pitter-patter of leaves,
A baby starting to cry.

Owls, wind and rain,
I listen to everything,
Every noisy passing car,
The flaps of birds' wings.

Till morning wakes me up,
With its shiny light,
I play with my friend's pup,
But I still remember the noises of the night.

Molly Harris (9)
Helmshore Primary School

Night Noises

When I'm in bed,
I turn off the light.
I like to listen hard,
To the noises of the night.

I hear the wind whistling
And I watch the bat go by,
As I look out of my window
And see trees growing high.

I hear cats on the garden fence,
Singing loud and clear,
As dogs begin to bark at them,
It seems like all year.

Cars go past my window,
And birds tap on the roof,
I hear snoring from the other room,
And owls go *hoot, hoot, hoot.*

And when I'm in bed,
I turn off the light,
And I like to listen hard,
To the noises of the night.

Tabitha Cross (10)
Helmshore Primary School

Night Noises

Lying in bed,
Everyone is fast asleep,
I don't sleep till ten,
I don't dream of sheep.

I hear noises on the roads,
I hear noises in the streets,
The trees are rustling
While all the birds tweet.

The cars are zooming past
And the owls in the park
Are hooting very loud
And they make the dogs bark.

The rain is falling down
On the window ledge,
I can hear the kids having fun
Getting ready with their sledge.

I am very tired now
And I need to get to sleep
But I don't sleep till ten
And I don't dream of sheep.

Olivia Harrison (10)
Helmshore Primary School

Noises Of The Night

Whilst I'm in bed at night,
There's lots to be heard,
Although those things are usually different,
From butterflies to birds.

The *vroom-vroom* of a passing car,
The snoring of my dad,
When the dog stops barking,
It really makes me glad.

Owls hooting loudly,
Cannot be missed at all,
The rustling sound of bush leaves,
Climbing up the wall.

The whooshing of the wind is loud,
Cats scratching at the door
And when the window's open,
I hear rain dripping on the floor.

When I'm awake in the day,
There's too much noise to be heard,
Night noises aren't as boring
As butterflies and birds.

Ashleigh Brooks (10)
Helmshore Primary School

When I'm In Bed

When I'm in bed
And all the light is dead,
It's quite a fright
When there is no light at night.

All I hear is my sister's snoring,
I cannot get to sleep, it is boring.
I hear the rain crashing down
And when I get no sleep I start to frown.

I'm bored, tired and awake,
I'm starting to feel like an earthquake.
I'm tired and sad,
Soon I'm going to go mad!

I look at the clock - twelve o'clock,
I peep out of the window,
I see sheep,
I have to get some sleep!

Tom Cross (10)
Helmshore Primary School

Night Noises

In the middle of the night,
I lie in bed
Listening to the owls hooting,
The trees rustling,
The wind howling
And the dogs barking.
My neighbours' cats fight and hiss
Although it's the middle of the night.

I lie in bed listening to the noises,
Though my sister makes horrible little baby noises,
The birds upon the roof,
The horses clanking with their hooves,
People walking down the path in shoes.

It's still the middle of the night,
But I'm tired now, so goodnight.

Laura Alice Jackson (10)
Helmshore Primary School

Night Noises

When I am trying to get to sleep,
There are lots of noises.
There are lots of different noises,
The noises of the night.

Sometimes I hear banging,
I don't know what it is.
I always hear cars
Slowly driving past.

My brother and sister are always snoring,
Sometimes the rain taps on the window.

When I am trying to get to sleep,
There are lots of noises.
There are lots of different noises,
The noises of the night.

Jack Tiler (10)
Helmshore Primary School

Night Noises

When I am lying in bed,
I hear cats miaowing in the night,
I just like to lie and listen
To the bats screeching in flight.

The *ding, ding, ding* of the rain,
The badgers scurrying up the hills,
I listen, listen and listen
To the clang of the mill.

Horses neighing all night long,
Owls hooting rapidly.
I listen while I'm lying
To the clock that goes *ding, dang, dong*.

Stars twinkling bright
In the corner of the night.
I lie and listen
To the silent aeroplane in flight.

All day I'm good,
People say I am a golden star of light
But I love to lie and listen
To the noises of the night.

Elizabeth Hollberry-Goddard (10)
Helmshore Primary School

Night Noises

When I'm in bed,
Trying to get some sleep,
I hear people across the road,
Throwing bottles in piles on heaps.

I hear rain on the roof,
And birds too.
I hear the wind whistling
And the owls hoot, hoot.

I hear the cars zooming,
Amongst the people walking.
The cars are extremely loud,
Amongst the people talking.

I hear my dad snoring,
Whilst he is in bed
And I hear my neighbour's cat miaow
Whilst being fed.

I hear the trees rustling,
I hear my friend's dog barking,
I hear rabbits scurrying
And the sound of cars parking.

I hear the sound of foxes
That are giving me a fright.
And these are the noises,
I hear in the night.

Katie Kendall (9)
Helmshore Primary School

Night Noises

When I am lying down
All settled in my bed,
Where everywhere is quiet
But also silently dead.

Animals come out,
Owls hoot, foxes scramble,
Bats squeak, dogs bark
And all the birds are tucked away nibbling.

Trees whistling in the night,
The wind strongly blowing,
All the lights switched off,
And the lamp post is left glowing.

People are loudly snoring,
Cars zooming by *vrooming*.
People walking and talking
Waking everyone up by singing and humming.

The night is bare,
Clear and dark,
Frightening and black
In the peaceful park.

Selene Bridge (10)
Helmshore Primary School

Night Noise

When I'm about to slumber
And the sun is not shining
I lie there and listen . . .
To those night noises.

I can hear people
I know that they're walking.
No, are they? Yes they are,
I can hear that they're talking.

The trees are tall,
But I can hear all,
With a rustle, rustle there
I can hear them on the moor.

I hear the sound of motors
Zooming down the hill,
It could be a van or a car,
Who knows, somebody will.

It is so black and still
A bat cannot be seen,
Only the light of street lights
Can be seen on these nights
But only the bats' squeals can be heard.

And then all the noises
Are suddenly gone.
It's wonderful to lie there listening . . .
To those night noises.

Nick Cooper (10)
Helmshore Primary School

Night Noises

When I'm in bed,
I hear strange noises.
Cars rushing past,
And the time going really fast.

It is weird,
My brother is snoring.
I can hear the cats miaowing
Now that can be extremely boring.

The sound of rain
Going *tap, tap, tap*.
The alarm clock ringing again
And the dogs barking.

The noises of loud voices,
The parties going *boom, boom, boom*.
The mice and rats scurrying for food
And my room is very gloomy.

When I'm in bed,
I hear strange noises.
They keep me awake
But I like to lie and listen.

Hannah Lundberg-Bury (10)
Helmshore Primary School

Night Noises

When I try to get to sleep in bed,
I just lie there and listen to the night go on.
I hear the cars going by
And I sit up and wait until the morn is upon.

I hear noises,
It sounds like a deer,
It reminds me of being on Blackpool Pier.

It is very, very strange,
I can hear my brother snoring,
I can hear drunk people,
That can be very boring.

The strange sound of the rain,
Tap, tap, tap.
I hear my neighbour walking her dog
The rain must sting her lap.

When I lie in my bed,
I can hear the birds in my roof tweeting.
I put my head on the pillow,
In my bed I hear my dog barking.
Then when I nod off
I can rest my head.

Lauren Watson (9)
Helmshore Primary School

Night Noises

When I am asleep
On my bed,
These are the noises
I hear in my head.

I hear noises
Like noisy cats
Going *miaow*,
But I don't like cats.

I hear cars going *vroom*,
When they are going down the road.
I can see something,
I think it is a toad.

I can hear the trees
In the wind,
My next-door neighbour
Looking for her cats.

I can hear my brother snoring
When he is in his room.
I can hear a car
Going *vroom!*

Connor Walsh (9)
Helmshore Primary School

Noises In The Night

When I'm tucked up in bed
And the moon is shining down,
There's many noises I can hear
When most people are asleep.

I can hear the creaking of the floorboards,
And the fighting of my cats,
I can hear the quiet hooting of an owl
Who is upon the oak tree.

I can hear the plodding of hedgehogs,
And the croaking of a frog,
I can hear the sound of footsteps
Walking down my close.

I can hear rabbits burrowing around
And making little tutting noises,
I can hear birds walking on the roof
And making sweet noises.

When I'm tucked up in bed
And the moon is shining down,
There are many noises I can hear
When most people are asleep.

Kim Smith (10)
Helmshore Primary School

Night Noises

When I'm in bed
I can hear,
The rustling of leaves
And rattling of trees.
When the wind blows
And my light glows
I can hear
The clinking of glasses.
I can hear
It all in my ear.
People are shouting,
Cats are miaowing,
When I'm in bed!

Matthew Densfield (10)
Helmshore Primary School

Night Noises

When I'm in bed,
There is tapping from the rain,
Snoring from my dad,
And a hooting train.

The wind whistling,
People walking and talking,
Trees banging on my window
And my mum who keeps on walking.

All I can hear is my brother talking
And him snoring,
The toilet flushing
And my window banging.

Cats and dogs
Barking and miaowing.
Scratching my head,
And scratching my feet.

When I'm in bed,
These are the little noises
Going around my head.

Lauren Haworth (9)
Helmshore Primary School

Night Noises

When I'm on my boat,
And there are lots of sounds to hear,
I love to lie and listen,
And I hear it every year.

I hear the water go *plonk, plonk, plonk,*
As the pontoon is creaking,
The seagulls' wings go flapping,
Whilst everyone is sleeping.

As people go past each minute,
As boats come in and out,
As I lie dreaming,
Oh I'd love to catch a trout.

In daytime it's so familiar
But at night it seems not real.
Sometimes it is so freaky,
But it is the real deal.

The noises are so weird,
As there isn't any light.
I like to listen hard
To the noises of the night.

Elspeth Lord (9)
Helmshore Primary School

Night Noises

When I am lying in bed
I lie and listen
To what is going on
In the dark sky.

I hear a cat miaowing
Upon my windowpane.
I hear a party going on
Next door to celebrate.

I hear my dad snoring,
It is really, really annoying.
I cannot hear
The *pitter-patter* of rain
Over my dad's loud snoring.

I hear the cars *vroom*
Past my window
As I pop my head
On my comfy pillow
And drift off to sleep.

Harriet Carruthers (9)
Helmshore Primary School

Night Noises

When I go to bed
I listen to night noises.
I hear the cars
Go *vroom!*

Snap, snap, snap, the twigs snap
When the squirrel goes to get nuts for supper.
Tap, tap, tap,
When the water falls off the gutter.

I hear the trees swaying in the wind,
I hear the rain bouncing off the windows,
Dogs howling and owls hooting;
And these are the night noises.

Toby Kay (10)
Helmshore Primary School

Night Noises

As I am in bed, wide awake,
I listen to the dawn of the day.
I sat up and get out of bed
To see my dad snoring in bed.

My dog is three,
She sleeps on the settee.
And when we're all in bed
She scratches on my bed.
I tiptoe downstairs to get a drink.

I hear croaking in the kitchen sink
So I go to get my dad
Who then gets extremely mad.
'Don't you dare wake me up again,
Or you won't see the light of day!'

Millie Keys (9)
Helmshore Primary School

Night Noises

I'm in my bed and I can hear
Bats squawking in the sky.
They are searching for food in the dark.
I hear owls in the trees hooting, but why?

I'm in my bed and I can hear
Cars driving fast,
The engines making loud noises.
Sometimes mice scuttle around
And sometimes I can see bats.

I'm in my bed and I can hear
Buses on the street beeping at cars.
Some hedgehogs creeping into gardens.
I don't want to do my chores.

I'm in my bed tucked up listening,
I am listening to all the animals,
They are all making different sounds
As I try to drift off.

Zak Drake (10)
Helmshore Primary School

Night Noises

When I'm in bed,
Sometimes I hear cars,
My cats miaow when I try to sleep.
Once I heard a dog barking.
My mum couldn't sleep.
Once it was really windy,
It turned the bins over.

John Stuart (10)
Helmshore Primary School

Happiness

H appiness is a bright sparkling sun
A bright sunny day
P irates sailing in the sea
P arties with my friends in the park
I am playing on my PS2 with my friends
N ice children smiling at me
E njoying swimming in the swimming pool on holiday
S un shining brightly down
S andy beach with people relaxing.

Morgan Bacon (8)
Helmshore Primary School

Happiness

H appiness is . . .
A bright sunny day with children
P eople playing in the park
P arties with my family
I ce cream melting in the sun
N ice sunny days
E xciting presents at Christmas
S un shining on people
S undays, a day before school.

Harry Yates (8)
Helmshore Primary School

Happiness

H appiness is . . .
A happy day on the beach
P resents under the lit up tree
P eople at the fair having fun
I ce pops on the beach
N ice cold water ready to drink
E xciting games ready to play
S omeone here having fun
S omeone going to the beach.

George Carpenter (7)
Helmshore Primary School

Sadness

S adness is . . .
A person crying
D olphins losing their way
N aughty people playing tricks
E ggs getting cracked
S ad people sitting down
S eagulls pinching chocolate ice cream.

Hannah Thornton (8)
Helmshore Primary School

Happiness

H appiness is . . .
A beautiful bright rainbow in the sky.
P resents under the Christmas tree.
P laying with my four best friends.
I ce cream with a flake for me!
N ice smells of roses all around.
E njoy your time playing with me.
S eeing dolphins in the sea.
S wimming in the crowded pool.

Heidi Wilson (8)
Helmshore Primary School

Happiness

H appiness is . . .
A beautiful princess playing a beautiful song
P retty poppies growing nice and red
P resents on your birthday
I n your Christmas stocking yo-yos
N ests and you are holding pretty chicks
E aster has finally arrived
S illy clowns feeling dizzy
S mall birds ready to hatch.

Sarah Jessica Russell (8)
Helmshore Primary School

Happiness

H appiness is . . .
A person in the sea
P eople having a party
P eople playing in the park
I n the sea is a big wave
N ice ice cream makes me happy
E agles flying in the sky
S ome people playing in the trees
S un smiling down on people.

Josef Ratcliffe (8)
Helmshore Primary School

Happiness

H appiness is . . .
A big bunch of balloons
P laying with your best friends
P arties with your family
I ce cream on a hot summer's day
N ice golden sun
E xcellent birthday presents
S eeing your friends at school
S troking your favourite cat.

Amy Mastyla (7)
Helmshore Primary School

Happiness

H appiness is . . .
A nger is never to be seen
P enguins sliding on the ice into the sea
P resents all lovely, wrapped and clean
I n books you see princesses and queens
N aughty monkeys playing tricks
E nchanted ocean, what could it be?
S hells in the sea chattering after me
S trawberries in a bowl with sugar on top.

Courtney Lord (8)
Helmshore Primary School

Happiness

H appiness is . . .
A nice day with your friends
P ets crawling on the floor
P resents still there from Christmas Eve
I ce pops still not eaten
N ests in a tree, where birds are singing
E ven monkeys climbing trees
S eeing the dolphins splashing around
S wimming in the sea.

Mollie Haynes (8)
Helmshore Primary School

Happiness!

H appiness is . . .
A bird in the sky
P resents in a box
P eople riding on a horse
I ce cream on the beach
N ice people playing on the beach
E nchanting films kids can watch
S eeing rabbits on the grass
S inging in the town!

Courtney Hardman (7)
Helmshore Primary School

Happiness

H appiness is . . .
A person having fun
P eople going to school
P rinces getting married
I ce cubes floating
N ice people making friends
E xcellent things coming true
S ea creatures being good
S omeone being nice.

Josh Haddy (8)
Helmshore Primary School

Sadness

S adness is . . .
A ddicted to drugs
D rinking lots of booze
N ice plants dying
E aster eggs have been eaten
S nakes are poisoning people
S adly the rain falls.

Jamie Gamble (8)
Helmshore Primary School

Excitement

Excitement is . . .
eX cited children playing in the park
C old ice cream being licked from head to toe
I ll people who are now feeling better
T he sea swaying to and fro
E xcitement spreading all over the world
M oney that you have won
E xciting clown coming to town
N umber one at horse riding
T V is on, let's watch something.

Erin Dempsey-McWade (7)
Helmshore Primary School

Happiness

H appiness is . . .
A bright sunny day
P eople playing cricket
P laying football
I ce cream on a hot day
N ice friends playing in the sand
E xciting people come to town
S eeing my family
S eeing planes fly in the sky.

Oliver Lord (8)
Helmshore Primary School

Happy Is . . .

H aving a bounce on a trampoline
A rriving in Spain
P laying with my friends
P laying with my racing cars
Y ummy, yummy ice cream!

Sean Frith (9)
Helmshore Primary School

Sadness

S adness is . . .
A thug drowning a dog in the water
D ad leaving home forever
N o one playing with you
E veryone bullying you
S harks ripping your legs off
S eeing someone in your family die.

Fraser Chapman (8)
Helmshore Primary School

Anger

A nger is
N eptune is angry at the sea
G ladiators fighting around the arena
E gg of a deadly dinosaur hatching
R aging rhino running across the road.

Daniel Rice (8)
Helmshore Primary School

Love

Love feels like a red silk ribbon circling around my heart,
It looks like a pale pink rose ready to blossom,
It sounds like a hummingbird humming softly,
It reminds me of an angel hovering over a bed.

Love sounds like sea waves rushing around the shore,
It tastes like a red juicy cherry ready to burst,
It feels like a soft, silky, comfy furry cushion,
It smells like a soft fragrant scented rose.

Chloe Geraghty (10)
Orrell Lamberhead Green CP School

Anger

Anger is like a burning ball inside.
It feels like a volcano busting on you.
It tastes like the hottest vindaloo in the world.
It sounds like a hammer smashing a building.
It looks like a burning flame around me.
It reminds me of bad memories.
It smells like a gas.

Connor Johnson (10)
Orrell Lamberhead Green CP School

Dogs

Dogs are cuddly and soft.
Dogs feel like a feather tickling you.
Dogs remind you of a fireball.
Dogs look like a furry carpet.
Dogs sound like a howling wolf.

Alix Carr (10)
Orrell Lamberhead Green CP School

Anger

Anger feels like a burning ball inside.
It smells like burning smoke.
It tastes like vindaloo.
It reminds you of bad memories.
It sounds like a screaming mouse.
It looks like an exploding volcano.
This is my poem about anger.

David Fagan (10)
Orrell Lamberhead Green CP School

I Love You So!

Sadness is like deep dark, dangerous blue.
Inside it tastes like my throat has sunk into my stomach.
It looks like a river of tears in front of my eyes.
It sounds like screams of death running past my heavy chest.
It feels like soft fur rubbing against my hair.
It smells like the scent of rot on my rabbit's plant pot.
It reminds me of the loss of Cuddles-Cuddles the rabbit.
I love you.

Shannon Hurley (10)
Orrell Lamberhead Green CP School

My Fluffy Dog Bluey

My dog is fluffy as a lion's mane.
He's as soft as a fly.
His blue and brown eyes twinkle like stars.
His claws are as sharp as steel knives.
His teeth are like white pearls.
His tail is as fluffy as a brush.
He runs like the wind.
He chases his ball, while I throw it off the wall.
And that is my dog Bluey.

Callum Taylor (9)
Orrell Lamberhead Green CP School

Cuddles The Rabbit

My rabbit cuddles is the best.
I play with him and I never need a rest,
I never shout at him if he eats my cress.

But now he has gone, there is no fun.

When he went it broke my heart,
But there's a lot of love for him in me.
Even now he's gone I love him
And that will never change.

Jade Hurley (10)
Orrell Lamberhead Green CP School

The Horse Prints

Clip-clop, clip-clop goes the animal that's wild.
Its heart is beating fast like a beating drum,
As it runs through a wood,
It runs on paths and grass,
It eats grain, it is always happy.
You can find them on farms and in fields.
Can you guess what animal it can be?

Georgia King (10)
Orrell Lamberhead Green CP School

Untitled

Middy, you lap milk super-fast
And you always have in the past.

Smokey-Joe
Sometimes tries to go
Ho, ho!

They both lap milk
As if they think it is silk.

As Misty, even though you are dead,
Your grave is in the flower bed.

Now our Thomas, says Nelly
Has a big belly.

Peppy preferred it when she was on her own
And now she will moan and groan.

Andrew Morris (10)
Orrell Lamberhead Green CP School

Anger

Anger is the colour of dark red flames.
Anger is the sound of an erupting volcano.
Anger tastes like a red-hot flaming curry.
Anger looks like a pair of devil's eyes.
Anger smells like fiery smoke drifting in the air.

Jack Boyle (9)
Orrell Lamberhead Green CP School

My Teacher Mrs Liptrot . . .

Is brainy,
Is cool,
Is fantastic,
Is the best,
Is good,
Is kind,
Is the assistant head teacher.
Mrs Liptrot is my teacher.

Michael Jones (10)
Orrell Lamberhead Green CP School

Cookies

Cookies are great.
Cookies are yum.
Cookies are fabulous,
Down in my tum.

I like to bake
But especially to eat.
Eating the cookies
Is a really big treat.

There are all sort of cookies,
Smartie ones,
Chocolate chip
And the macaroons.

I've no idea what
Macaroons are
But they sound nice.
I don't know why,
But I might make them twice.

There's only one thing
Those cookies can't beat,
It's the packets and packets
Of really big sweets.

I love all sweets
And I'm sure you do,
The chewies and suckers
Are the best too.

Cookies are lovely
We all think they're yum.
But you really have to watch
The size of your tum.

Nicole Amy Wilson (10)
Pinfold Primary School

Hockey

I play for Phoenix, I'm in goal.
I'm getting ready to play for my team.
I love playing hockey, especially in net.
There's a girl in the team - the hockey queen.

I make a stick save, and the puck drops to the ground.
The other team get the puck and they do a wrap around.

My helmet looks like a devil.
I have to wear a mask on my face,
But most of all
You have to tie up your lace.

Jake Daniel Higham (10)
Pinfold Primary School

My Brother

My little brother likes sweets,
His favourite is pick 'n' mix.
He like cherries and cola bottles
But his best is lolls on sticks.

My little brother likes chocolate,
He likes it a lot,
Even when it's runny
And even when it's hot.

My little brother has lots of pets,
Puppy dogs, a parrot and fish
He like his puppy dogs a lot,
But a turtle is his wish.

My brother like pets a lot,
He goes on Saturday to the pet store.
He always comes out with something different
But once he came out with four!

My little brother has curly-wurly hair,
Deep brown eyes and brownish skin.
He really is quite small,
It think he would fit in a tin.

Shevana Kent (9)
Pinfold Primary School

Size

A kilometre is like . . .
The Great Wall of China
The sky so far
As deep as the sea
And from here to the moon.

A metre is like . . .
The size of the Empire State Building
As green and as scary as an alligator
And as long as a snake.

A centimetre is like . . .
A lazy baby crying
A caterpillar eating a big green leaf.

Elliot Holt (8)
St Andrew's Over Hulton CE Primary School, Bolton

Jungle

Inside the strange jungle there is . . .
A ferocious, fast fire fox fainting
A weary, woeful, weird wolf
A slithery snake snacking
A live lion licking
A ticking tiger talking
A magical monkey making mischief
A chanting cheetah chewing
A peeking parrot panting
An enormous elephant eating.

Peter Gradwell (8)
St Andrew's Over Hulton CE Primary School, Bolton

Football Super Stars

Fantastic ugly Rooney always cheating
Ronaldo, skills with a ball, feet like lightning
Watch United go, goals every second,
Anelka slide tackles, shoots a cracker
Football fans sulk and pull out their hair
Juissie dives and catches the ball
They wear a maroon kit
Different people with microphone hair
Campo slides, red card, off!
Balls glimmering in the sunlight
Football is the best thing, shooting, booting every day!

Lucy Waddington (9)
St Andrew's Over Hulton CE Primary School, Bolton

Football - Cinquain

Football
Football is mad
Football's about winning
Football is rough, football is fast
Scoring.

Alex Latham (9)
St Andrew's Over Hulton CE Primary School, Bolton

Dependable

D elicious food that God made.
E veryone has trust in God.
P eople were made by God.
E veryone believes in God.
N ever give up on God.
D rinks and water were made by God.
A dam and Eve were first made by God.
B ranches and trees were made by God.
L ight and dark were made by God.
E very person matters to God.

Alex Cooper (9)
St Andrew's Over Hulton CE Primary School, Bolton

Inside The Jungle

Inside
African jungles
There are
Cool croaking cockroaches
Mad moving monkeys
Sound soothing snakes
Annoying aggravating alligators
Pointing poking parrots
Terrifying tiring tigers
Boring bouncing birds
Wild warring werewolves
Roaring rattling rats
Lovely loose lions
Enormous electrical elephants
Fantastic furry flamingos
Gigantic gorgeous gorillas
Hungry hunting horses.

Amy Grundy (9)
St Andrew's Over Hulton CE Primary School, Bolton

The Nasty Jungle

Inside
This
Nasty
Jungle
There lives
A slippery, slimy, scary snake
An orange-black, meat-eating, terrifying tiger
A dangerous banana-eating monkey
A scary panther with sharp teeth
A fuzzy, furious white rabbit
A brown, grizzly, loud, furry bear
A dazzling, dancing, horrible squeal
A terrible, terrifying, lonely lion
A big, green, nasty tortoise
A fantastic, flying, furious bat
Inside the nasty jungle.

Ellie Shawcross (9)
St Andrew's Over Hulton CE Primary School, Bolton

Deep In The Jungle

Deep down in the
Dangerous jungle is
A sloppy, slimy, slithering slug
A tipping, toppling, tripping tiger
A beautiful, buzzing, biting bee
A cocky, calling cross-eyed cockroach
A fantastic, fat, flipping fire ant
A silly, slapping, stupid slug
A super, snoring, sniffing snake.

Brandon Melia (9)
St Andrew's Over Hulton CE Primary School, Bolton

Size

A kilometre is like . . .
Along the hot desert
All around the world
As deep as the blue sea
And from here to the moon.

A metre is like . . .
The beautiful Statue of Liberty
All of the amazing Blackpool Tower
The slippery slime of a slug
And the length of the scaly snake.

A centimetre is like . . .
The height of a loud baby
The width of a wide book
The size of your hand span
And the measurement of a lovely butterfly.

A millimetre is like . . .
A little yellow bird's beak
The brushes of a small paintbrush
One tiny pink fingernail
And a little crunch chrysalis.

Rachel Peacock (9)
St Andrew's Over Hulton CE Primary School, Bolton

The Butterfly - Haiku

Beautiful bright wings
Bursting into colours, and
Floating through the wind.

Jasmine Delvard (9)
St Andrew's Over Hulton CE Primary School, Bolton

In The Jungle

Deep in the middle
Of the jungle there is
A brave bear growling
A giddy gruesome gorilla sleeping
A slimy, slippery snake hissing
A roaring lion licking its cub's fur
A lively, lazy monkey snoring
A deadly dinosaur eating its prey
A squeaky, squawky parrot spying
A tall spotty giraffe chewing trees
A squirmy white maggot crawling.

Amy Neill (9)
St Andrew's Over Hulton CE Primary School, Bolton

My Mum, Your Mum

My mum is cooler than your mum,
Oh yes, my mum is cooler alright.
She is a beautiful superstar,
Who stays out partying all night.

No, my mum is faster than your mum,
Yes my mum is faster that's true.
If my mum were here right now
She would run circles around you.

But my mum is smarter than your mum,
My mum is smarter OK.
She can do mental maths in a super flash,
So don't get in her way!

Wow, who cares? But my mum is more stylish than your mum,
My mum is like the stylish master.
If you keep getting in her way,
You will be covered head to toe in plaster.

Do you know what?
My mum does not care about me.

No neither does mine.
So how about we get together and go on a shopping spree.

Nicola Robinson (10)
St Francis of Assisi Primary School, Skelmersdale

Things I Like

I like the taste of chocolate.
I like the smell of tennis balls.
I like the feel of cotton wool.
I like the sound of cats.
I like the look of a roast dinner.

I like the feel of cats rubbing against my skin.
I like the taste of a roast dinner sizzling in my mouth.
I like the look of cotton wool, nice and warm.
I like the smell of chocolate melting in the sun.
I like the sound of tennis balls banging against a racket.

Andrew Moss (10)
St Francis of Assisi Primary School, Skelmersdale

All Around Me

I like the taste of ice lollies.
I like the smell of fresh air.
I like the feel of rose petals.
I like the sound of waves.
I like the look of colours.

I like the look of waves, smashing and crashing
                               against the rocks.
I like the taste of fresh air breathing in my face.
I like the smell of rose petals whizzing up my nose.
I like the sound of colours whispering around me.
I like the feel of ice lollies melting down the stick
                               in my hand.

Bethany Rimmet (9)
St Francis of Assisi Primary School, Skelmersdale

I Like

I like the taste of my mum's cooking.
I like the smell of my flowers.
I like the feel of wool.
I like the sound of music.
I like the look of fruit.

I like the look of wool, when I start knitting.
I like the sound of my flowers, shining in the summer sun.
I like the feel of music, drifting in the air around me.
I like the smell of my mum's cooking, when she cooks
                                        my favourite tea.
I like the taste of fruit, when I take a bite of it.

Courtney Rowlands (9)
St Francis of Assisi Primary School, Skelmersdale

I Like

I like the taste of ice cream.
I like the smell of a coal fire.
I like the feel of leather.
I like the sound of water.
I like the look of the wind.

I like the taste of water, running down my throat.
I like the smell of ice cream, melting in the sun.
I like the feel of a coal fire, brushing against my skin.
I like the sound of the wind, blowing ever so silently.
I like the look of leather, crinkling when sat on.

Matthew Wise (9)
St Francis of Assisi Primary School, Skelmersdale

Senses

I like the taste of jelly.
I like the smell of shampoo.
I like the feel of cut grass.
I like the sound of rain.
I like the look of a dog's fur.

I like the look of jelly, wobbling on a plate.
I like the feel of a dog's fur, rubbing on my hand.
I like the sound of shampoo bubbling in my ears.
I like the smell of cut grass, fragrant in the summer breeze.
I like the taste of rain, dropping in my mouth.

Emma Millar (9)
St Francis of Assisi Primary School, Skelmersdale

I Like

I like the taste of chocolate sauce.
I like the smell of pineapple.
I like the feel of silk.
I like the sound of rain.
I like the look of colours.

I like the taste of pineapple juice down my throat.
I like the smell of silk, perfumed in my nostrils.
I like the feel of chocolate sauce, pouring through my fingers.
I like the sound of colours echoing around me.
I like the look of rain, pounding on the ground.

Abbey Cash-Francis (10)
St Francis of Assisi Primary School, Skelmersdale

Winter

Winter has a lovely breeze
out in the air as fresh as can be
cold but happy
sitting by the fire.

    Everything goes dark
    wearing scarves, gloves and hats
    drinking hot chocolate
    sitting by the fire.

        The clouds go black
        the trees go bare
        we get shivers
        in the cold night air.

Faeema Kakuji (11)
St Matthews CE Primary School, Bolton

Winter

W ater turns to icicles, fogginess and dust.
I cy ice rinks at the park, don't skate there, it's a must.
N ever open the window, or you'll get a snowball in your face.
T rust me, never give a snowman your tooth brace.
E xamples for weather are not sunny, in fact they're very bad.
R ain and sleet, snow and wind, or course will make you sad.

W hen you sit beside the fire to warm your frosty toes
I cy snow for a snowman's head and a carrot for his nose.
N ice warm soup to warm your body,
T rifle for dessert,
E ven statues feel chilly,
R ock about and watch the telly, sipping hot chocolate held by hands full of dirt.

Liam Conroy (10)
St Matthews CE Primary School, Bolton

Young Writers Information

We hope you have enjoyed reading this book - and that you will continue to enjoy it in the coming years.

If you like reading and writing poetry drop us a line, or give us a call, and we'll send you a free information pack.

Alternatively if you would like to order further copies of this book or any of our other titles, then please give us a call or log onto our website at
www.youngwriters.co.uk

Young Writers Information
Remus House
Coltsfoot Drive
Peterborough
PE2 9JX

(01733) 890066